The Mob by John Galsworthy

A Play in Four Acts

Third Series Plays

John Galsworthy was born at Kingston Upon Thames in Surrey, England, on August 14th 1867 to a wealthy and well established family. His schooling was at Harrow and New College, Oxford before training as a barrister and being called to the bar in 1890. However, Law was not attractive to him and he travelled abroad becoming great friends with the novelist Joseph Conrad, then a first mate on a sailing ship.

In 1895 Galsworthy began an affair with Ada Nemesis Pearson Cooper, the wife of his cousin Major Arthur Galsworthy. The affair was kept a secret for 10 years till she at last divorced and they married on 23 September 1905.

John Galsworthy first published in 1897 with a collection of short stories entitled "The Four Winds". For the next 7 years he published these and all works under his pen name John Sinjohn. It was only upon the death of his father and the publication of "The Island Pharisees" in 1904 that he published as John Galsworthy. In this volume we have Villa Rubein ays and studies. They are the work of a supreme talent at the top of his game. Whilst today he is far more well know as a Nobel Prize winning novelist then he was considered a playwright dealing with social issues and the class system. He was appointed to the Order of Merit in 1929, after earlier turning down a knighthood, and awarded the Nobel Prize in 1932 though he was too ill to attend. John Galsworthy died from a brain tumour at his London home, Grove Lodge, Hampstead on January 31st 1933. In accordance with his will he was cremated at Woking with his ashes then being scattered over the South Downs from an aeroplane.

He is now far better known for his novels, particularly The Forsyte Saga, his trilogy about the eponymous family of the same name. These books, as with many of his other works, deal with social class, upper-middle class lives in particular. Although always sympathetic to his characters, he reveals their insular, snobbish, and somewhat greedy attitudes and suffocating moral codes. He is now viewed as one of the first from the Edwardian era to challenge some of the ideals of society depicted in the literature of Victorian England.

In his writings he campaigns for a variety of causes, including prison reform, women's rights, animal welfare, and the opposition of censorship as well as a recurring theme of an unhappy marriage from the women's side. During World War I he worked in a hospital in France as an orderly after being passed over for military service.

He was appointed to the Order of Merit in 1929, after earlier turning down a knighthood, and awarded the Nobel Prize in 1932 though he was too ill to attend.

John Galsworthy died from a brain tumour at his London home, Grove Lodge, Hampstead on January 31st 1933. In accordance with his will he was cremated at Woking with his ashes then being scattered over the South Downs from an aeroplane.

Index of Contents

PERSONS OF THE PLAY

STEPHEN MORE, Member of Parliament
KATHERINE, his wife
OLIVE, their little daughter
THE DEAN OF STOUR, Katherine's uncle
GENERAL SIR JOHN JULIAN, her father
CAPTAIN HUBERT JULIAN, her brother
HELEN, his wife
EDWARD MENDIP, editor of "The Parthenon"
ALAN STEEL, More's secretary
JAMES HOME, architect   }
CHARLES SHELDER, Solicitor   } A deputation of More's
MARK WACE, bookseller   } constituents
WILLIAM BANNING, manufacturer   }
NURSE WREFORD
WREFORD (her son), Hubert's orderly
HIS SWEETHEART
THE FOOTMAN HENRY
A DOORKEEPER
SOME BLACK-COATED GENTLEMEN
A STUDENT
A GIRL

Between ACTS I and II some days elapse.
Between ACTS II and III three months.
Between ACT III SCENE I and ACT III SCENE II no time.
Between ACTS III and IV a few hours.
Between ACTS IV and AFTERMATH an indefinite period.

ACT I

It is half-past nine of a July evening. In a dining-room lighted by sconces, and apparelled in wall-paper, carpet, and curtains of deep vivid blue, the large French windows between two columns are open on to a wide terrace, beyond which are seen trees in darkness, and distant shapes of lighted houses. On one side is a bay window, over which curtains are partly drawn. Opposite to this window is a door leading into the hall. At an oval rosewood table, set with silver, flowers, fruit, and wine, six people are seated after dinner. Back to the bay window is **STEPHEN MORE**, the host, a man of forty, with a fine-cut face, a rather charming smile, and the eyes of an idealist; to his right, **SIR, JOHN JULIAN**, an old soldier, with thin brown features, and grey moustaches; to Sir John's right, his brother, the **DEAN OF STOUR**, a tall, dark, ascetic-looking Churchman: to his right **KATHERINE** is leaning forward, her elbows on the table, and her chin on her hands, staring across at her husband; to her right sits **EDWARD MENDIP**, a pale man of forty-five, very bald, with a fine forehead, and on his clear-cut lips a smile that shows his teeth; between him and **MORE** is **HELEN JULIAN**, a pretty dark-haired young woman, absorbed in thoughts of her own. The voices are tuned to the pitch of heated discussion, as the curtain rises.

THE DEAN
I disagree with you, Stephen; absolutely, entirely disagree.

MORE
I can't help it.

MENDIP
Remember a certain war, Stephen! Were your chivalrous notions any good, then? And, what was winked at in an obscure young Member is anathema for an Under Secretary of State. You can't afford—

MORE
To follow my conscience? That's new, Mendip.

MENDIP
Idealism can be out of place, my friend.

THE DEAN
The Government is dealing here with a wild lawless race, on whom I must say I think sentiment is rather wasted.

MORE
God made them, Dean.

MENDIP
I have my doubts.

THE DEAN
They have proved themselves faithless. We have the right to chastise.

MORE
If I hit a little man in the eye, and he hits me back, have I the right to chastise him?

SIR JOHN

We didn't begin this business.

MORE

What! With our missionaries and our trading?

THE DEAN

It is news indeed that the work of civilization may be justifiably met by murder. Have you forgotten Glaive and Morlinson?

SIR JOHN

Yes. And that poor fellow Groome and his wife?

MORE

They went into a wild country, against the feeling of the tribes, on their own business. What has the nation to do with the mishaps of gamblers?

SIR JOHN

We can't stand by and see our own flesh and blood ill-treated!

THE DEAN

Does our rule bring blessing—or does it not, Stephen?

MORE

Sometimes; but with all my soul I deny the fantastic superstition that our rule can benefit a people like this, a nation of one race, as different from ourselves as dark from light—in colour, religion, every mortal thing. We can only pervert their natural instincts.

THE DEAN

That to me is an unintelligible point of view.

MENDIP

Go into that philosophy of yours a little deeper, Stephen—it spells stagnation. There are no fixed stars on this earth. Nations can't let each other alone.

MORE

Big ones could let little ones alone.

MENDIP

If they could there'd be no big ones. My dear fellow, we know little nations are your hobby, but surely office should have toned you down.

SIR JOHN

I've served my country fifty years, and I say she is not in the wrong.

MORE

I hope to serve her fifty, Sir John, and I say she is.

MENDIP

There are moments when such things can't be said, More.

MORE

They'll be said by me to-night, Mendip.

MENDIP

In the House?

[**MORE** nods.

KATHERINE

Stephen!

MENDIP

Mrs. More, you mustn't let him. It's madness.

MORE [Rising]

You can tell people that to-morrow, Mendip. Give it a leader in 'The Parthenon'.

MENDIP

Political lunacy! No man in your position has a right to fly out like this at the eleventh hour.

MORE

I've made no secret of my feelings all along. I'm against this war, and against the annexation we all know it will lead to.

MENDIP

My dear fellow! Don't be so Quixotic! We shall have war within the next twenty-four hours, and nothing you can do will stop it.

HELEN

Oh! No!

MENDIP

I'm afraid so, Mrs. Hubert.

SIR JOHN

Not a doubt of it, Helen.

MENDIP [To **MORE**]

And you mean to charge the windmill?

[**MORE** nods.

MENDIP

'C'est magnifique'!

MORE
I'm not out for advertisement.

MENDIP
You will get it!

MORE
Must speak the truth sometimes, even at that risk.

SIR JOHN
It is not the truth.

MENDIP
The greater the truth the greater the libel, and the greater the resentment of the person libelled.

THE DEAN [Trying to bring matters to a blander level]
My dear Stephen, even if you were right—which I deny—about the initial merits, there surely comes a point where the individual conscience must resign it self to the country's feeling. This has become a question of national honour.

SIR JOHN
Well said, James!

MORE
Nations are bad judges of their honour, Dean.

THE DEAN
I shall not follow you there.

MORE
No. It's an awkward word.

KATHERINE [Stopping **THE DEAN**]
Uncle James! Please!

[**MORE** looks at her intently.

SIR JOHN
So you're going to put yourself at the head of the cranks, ruin your career, and make me ashamed that you're my son-in-law?

MORE
Is a man only to hold beliefs when they're popular? You've stood up to be shot at often enough, Sir John.

SIR JOHN
Never by my country! Your speech will be in all the foreign press-trust 'em for seizing on anything against us. A show-up before other countries—!

MORE
You admit the show-up?

SIR JOHN
I do not, sir.

THE DEAN
The position has become impossible. The state of things out there must be put an end to once for all! Come, Katherine, back us up!

MORE
My country, right or wrong! Guilty—still my country!

MENDIP
That begs the question.

[**KATHERINE** rises. **THE DEAN**, too, stands up.

THE DEAN [In a low voice]
'Quem Deus volt perdere'—!

SIR JOHN
Unpatriotic!

MORE
I'll have no truck with tyranny.

KATHERINE
Father doesn't admit tyranny. Nor do any of us, Stephen.

[**HUBERT JULIAN**, a tall Soldier-like man, has come in.

HELEN
Hubert!

[She gets up and goes to him, and they talk together near the door.

SIR JOHN
What in God's name is your idea? We've forborne long enough, in all conscience.

MORE
Sir John, we great Powers have got to change our ways in dealing with weaker nations. The very dogs can give us lessons—watch a big dog with a little one.

MENDIP
No, no, these things are not so simple as all that.

MORE

There's no reason in the world, Mendip, why the rules of chivalry should not apply to nations at least as well as to—dogs.

MENDIP

My dear friend, are you to become that hapless kind of outcast, a champion of lost causes?

MORE

This cause is not lost.

MENDIP

Right or wrong, as lost as ever was cause in all this world. There was never a time when the word "patriotism" stirred mob sentiment as it does now. 'Ware "Mob," Stephen—'ware "Mob"!

MORE

Because general sentiment's against me, I—a public man—am to deny my faith? The point is not whether I'm right or wrong, Mendip, but whether I'm to sneak out of my conviction because it's unpopular.

THE DEAN

I'm afraid I must go. [To **KATHERINE**] Good-night, my dear! Ah! Hubert!

[He greets **HUBERT**.

Mr. Mendip, I go your way. Can I drop you?

MENDIP

Thank you. Good-night, Mrs. More. Stop him! It's perdition.

[He and **THE DEAN** go out. **KATHERINE** puts her arm in **HELEN'S**, and takes her out of the room. **HUBERT** remains standing by the door.

SIR JOHN

I knew your views were extreme in many ways, Stephen, but I never thought the husband of my daughter would be a Peace-at-any-price man!

MORE

I am not! But I prefer to fight some one my own size.

SIR JOHN

Well! I can only hope to God you'll come to your senses before you commit the folly of this speech. I must get back to the War Office. Good-night, Hubert.

HUBERT

Good-night, Father.

[**SIR JOHN** goes out. **HUBERT** stands motionless, dejected.

HUBERT
We've got our orders.

MORE
What? When d'you sail?

HUBERT
At once.

MORE
Poor Helen!

HUBERT
Not married a year; pretty bad luck!

[**MORE** touches his arm in sympathy.

Well! We've got to put feelings in our pockets. Look here, Stephen—don't make that speech! Think of Katherine—with the Dad at the War Office, and me going out, and Ralph and old George out there already! You can't trust your tongue when you're hot about a thing.

MORE
I must speak, Hubert.

HUBERT
No, no! Bottle yourself up for to-night. The next few hours 'll see it begin. [**MORE** turns from him] If you don't care whether you mess up your own career—don't tear Katherine in two!

MORE
You're not shirking your duty because of your wife.

HUBERT
Well! You're riding for a fall, and a godless mucker it'll be. This'll be no picnic. We shall get some nasty knocks out there. Wait and see the feeling here when we've had a force or two cut up in those mountains. It's awful country. Those fellows have got modern arms, and are jolly good fighters. Do drop it, Stephen!

MORE
Must risk something, sometimes, Hubert—even in my profession!

[As he speaks, **KATHERINE** comes in.

HUBERT
But it's hopeless, my dear chap—absolutely.

[**MORE** turns to the window, **HUBERT** to his sister—then with a gesture towards **MORE**, as though to leave the matter to her, he goes out.

KATHERINE

Stephen! Are you really going to speak? [He nods] I ask you not.

MORE

You know my feeling.

KATHERINE

But it's our own country. We can't stand apart from it. You won't stop anything—only make people hate you. I can't bear that.

MORE

I tell you, Kit, some one must raise a voice. Two or three reverses—certain to come—and the whole country will go wild. And one more little nation will cease to live.

KATHERINE

If you believe in your country, you must believe that the more land and power she has, the better for the world.

MORE

Is that your faith?

KATHERINE

Yes.

MORE

I respect it; I even understand it; but—I can't hold it.

KATHERINE

But, Stephen, your speech will be a rallying cry to all the cranks, and every one who has a spite against the country. They'll make you their figurehead. [**MORE** smiles] They will. Your chance of the Cabinet will go—you may even have to resign your seat.

MORE

Dogs will bark. These things soon blow over.

KATHERINE

No, no! If you once begin a thing, you always go on; and what earthly good?

MORE

History won't say: "And this they did without a single protest from their public men!"

KATHERINE

There are plenty who—

MORE

Poets?

KATHERINE

Do you remember that day on our honeymoon, going up Ben Lawers? You were lying on your face in the heather; you said it was like kissing a loved woman. There was a lark singing—you said that was the voice of one's worship. The hills were very blue; that's why we had blue here, because it was the best dress of our country. You do love her.

MORE
Love her!

KATHERINE
You'd have done this for me—then.

MORE
Would you have asked me—then, Kit?

KATHERINE
Yes. The country's our country! Oh! Stephen, think what it'll be like for me—with Hubert and the other boys out there. And poor Helen, and Father! I beg you not to make this speech.

MORE
Kit! This isn't fair. Do you want me to feel myself a cur?

KATHERINE [Breathless]
I—I—almost feel you'll be a cur to do it

[She looks at him, frightened by her own words. Then, as the footman **HENRY** has come in to clear the table—very low.

I ask you not!

[He does not answer, and she goes out.

MORE [To the **SERVANT**]
Later, please, Henry, later!

[The **SERVANT** retires. **MORE** still stands looking down at the dining-table; then putting his hand to his throat, as if to free it from the grip of his collar, he pours out a glass of water, and drinks it of. In the street, outside the bay window, two street musicians, a harp and a violin, have taken up their stand, and after some twangs and scrapes, break into music. **MORE** goes towards the sound, and draws aside one curtain. After a moment, he returns to the table, and takes up the notes of the speech. He is in an agony of indecision.

MORE
A cur!

[He seems about to tear his notes across. Then, changing his mind, turns them over and over, muttering. His voice gradually grows louder, till he is declaiming to the empty room the peroration of his speech.

MORE

.... We have arrogated to our land the title Champion of Freedom, Foe of Oppression. Is that indeed a bygone glory? Is it not worth some sacrifice of our pettier dignity, to avoid laying another stone upon its grave; to avoid placing before the searchlight eyes of History the spectacle of yet one more piece of national cynicism? We are about to force our will and our dominion on a race that has always been free, that loves its country, and its independence, as much as ever we love ours. I cannot sit silent to-night and see this begin. As we are tender of our own land, so we should be of the lands of others. I love my country. It is because I love my country that I raise my voice. Warlike in spirit these people may be— but they have no chance against ourselves. And war on such, however agreeable to the blind moment, is odious to the future. The great heart of mankind ever beats in sense and sympathy with the weaker. It is against this great heart of mankind that we are going. In the name of Justice and Civilization we pursue this policy; but by Justice we shall hereafter be judged, and by Civilization—condemned.

[While he is speaking, a little figure has flown along the terrace outside, in the direction of the music, but has stopped at the sound of his voice, and stands in the open window, listening—a dark-haired, dark-eyed child, in a blue dressing-gown caught up in her hand. The street musicians, having reached the end of a tune, are silent.

[In the intensity of **MORES** feeling, a wine-glass, gripped too strongly, breaks and falls in pieces onto a finger-bowl. The child starts forward into the room.

MORE
Olive!

OLIVE
Who were you speaking to, Daddy?

MORE [Staring at her]
The wind, sweetheart!

OLIVE
There isn't any!

MORE
What blew you down, then?

OLIVE [Mysteriously]
The music. Did the wind break the wine-glass, or did it come in two in your hand?

MORE
Now my sprite! Upstairs again, before Nurse catches you. Fly! Fly!

OLIVE
Oh! no, Daddy! [With confidential fervour] It feels like things to-night!

MORE
You're right there!

OLIVE [Pulling him down to her, and whispering]
I must get back again in secret. H'sh!

[She suddenly runs and wraps herself into one of the curtains of the bay window. A young **MAN** enters, with a note in his hand.

MORE
Hello, Steel!

[The street **MUSICIANS** have again begun to play.]

STEEL
From Sir John—by special messenger from the War Office.

MORE [Reading the note]
"The ball is opened."

[He stands brooding over the note, and **STEEL** looks at him anxiously. He is a dark, sallow, thin-faced young man, with the eyes of one who can attach himself to people, and suffer with them.

STEEL
I'm glad it's begun, sir. It would have been an awful pity to have made that speech.

MORE
You too, Steel!

STEEL
I mean, if it's actually started—

MORE [Tearing tie note across]
Yes. Keep that to yourself.

STEEL
Do you want me any more?

[**MORE** takes from his breast pocket some papers, and pitches them down on the bureau.

MORE
Answer these.

STEEL [Going to the bureau]
Fetherby was simply sickening.

[He begins to write. Struggle has begun again in **MORE**]

Not the faintest recognition that there are two sides to it.

[**MORE** gives him a quick look, goes quietly to the dining-table and picks up his sheaf of notes. Hiding them with his sleeve, he goes back to the window, where he again stands hesitating.

STEEL
Chief gem: [Imitating] "We must show Impudence at last that Dignity is not asleep!"

MORE [Moving out on to the terrace]
Nice quiet night!

STEEL
This to the Cottage Hospital—shall I say you will preside?

MORE
No.

[**STEEL** writes; then looking up and seeing that **MORE** is no longer there, he goes to the window, looks to right and left, returns to the bureau, and is about to sit down again when a thought seems to strike him with consternation. He goes again to the window. Then snatching up his hat, he passes hurriedly out along the terrace. As he vanishes, **KATHERINE** comes in from the hall. After looking out on to the terrace she goes to the bay window; stands there listening; then comes restlessly back into the room. **OLIVE**, creeping quietly from behind the curtain, clasps her round the waist.

KATHERINE
O my darling! How you startled me! What are you doing down here, you wicked little sinner!

OLIVE
I explained all that to Daddy. We needn't go into it again, need we?

KATHERINE
Where is Daddy?

OLIVE
Gone.

KATHERINE
When?

OLIVE
Oh! only just, and Mr. Steel went after him like a rabbit. [The music stops] They haven't been paid, you know.

KATHERINE
Now, go up at once. I can't think how you got down here.

OLIVE
I can. [Wheedling] If you pay them, Mummy, they're sure to play another.

KATHERINE

Well, give them that! One more only.

[She gives **OLIVE** a coin, who runs with it to the bay window, opens the aide casement, and calls to the musicians.

OLIVE
Catch, please! And would you play just one more?

[She returns from the window, and seeing her mother lost in thought, rubs herself against her.

OLIVE
Have you got an ache?

KATHARINE
Right through me, darling!

OLIVE
Oh!

[The musicians strike up a dance.

OLIVE
Oh! Mummy! I must just dance!

[She kicks off her lisle blue shoes, and begins dancing. While she is capering **HUBERT** comes in from the hall. He stands watching his little niece for a minute, and **KATHERINE** looks at him.

HUBERT
Stephen gone!

KATHERINE
Yes—stop, Olive!

OLIVE
Are you good at my sort of dancing, Uncle?

HUBERT
Yes, chick—awfully!

KATHERINE
Now, Olive!

[The musicians have suddenly broken off in the middle of a bar. From the street comes the noise of distant shouting.

OLIVE
Listen, Uncle! Isn't it a particular noise?

[HUBERT and KATHERINE listen with all their might, and OLIVE stares at their faces. HUBERT goes to the window. The sound comes nearer. The shouted words are faintly heard: "Pyper—war—our force crosses frontier—sharp fightin'—pyper."

KATHERINE [Breathless]
Yes! It is.

[The street cry is heard again in two distant voices coming from different directions: "War—pyper—sharp fightin' on the frontier—pyper."

KATHERINE
Shut out those ghouls!

[As HUBERT closes the window, NURSE WREFORD comes in from the hall. She is an elderly woman endowed with a motherly grimness. She fixes OLIVE with her eye, then suddenly becomes conscious of the street cry.

NURSE
Oh! don't say it's begun.

[HUBERT comes from the window.

NURSE
Is the regiment to go, Mr. Hubert?

HUBERT
Yes, Nanny.

NURSE
Oh, dear! My boy!

KATHERINE [Signing to where OLIVE stands with wide eyes]
Nurse!

HUBERT
I'll look after him, Nurse.

NURSE
And him keepin' company. And you not married a year. Ah! Mr. Hubert, now do 'ee take care; you and him's both so rash.

HUBERT
Not I, Nurse!

[NURSE looks long into his face, then lifts her finger, and beckons OLIVE.

OLIVE [Perceiving new sensations before her, goes quietly]

Good-night, Uncle! Nanny, d'you know why I was obliged to come down? [In a fervent whisper] It's a secret!

[As she passes with **NURSE** out into the hall, her voice is heard saying, "Do tell me all about the war."

HUBERT [Smothering emotion under a blunt manner]
We sail on Friday, Kit. Be good to Helen, old girl.

KATHERINE
Oh! I wish—! Why—can't—women—fight?

HUBERT
Yes, it's bad for you, with Stephen taking it like this. But he'll come round now it's once begun.

[**KATHERINE** shakes her head, then goes suddenly up to him, and throws her arms round his neck. It is as if all the feeling pent up in her were finding vent in this hug.

[The door from the hall is opened, and **SIR JOHN'S** voice is heard outside: "All right, I'll find her."

KATHERINE
Father!

[**SIR JOHN** comes in.

SIR JOHN
Stephen get my note? I sent it over the moment I got to the War Office.

KATHERINE
I expect so.

[Seeing the torn note on the table.

Yes.

SIR JOHN
They're shouting the news now. Thank God, I stopped that crazy speech of his in time.

KATHERINE
Have you stopped it?

SIR JOHN
What! He wouldn't be such a sublime donkey?

KATHERINE
I think that is just what he might be.

[Going to the window.

We shall know soon.

[SIR JOHN, after staring at her, goes up to HUBERT.

SIR JOHN
Keep a good heart, my boy. The country's first.

[They exchange a hand-squeeze.

[KATHERINE backs away from the window. STEEL has appeared there from the terrace, breathless from running.

STEEL
Mr. More back?

KATHERINE
No. Has he spoken?

STEEL
Yes.

KATHERINE
Against?

STEEL
Yes.

SIR JOHN
What? After!

[SIR, JOHN stands rigid, then turns and marches straight out into the hall. At a sign from KATHERINE, HUBERT follows him.

KATHERINE
Yes, Mr. Steel?

STEEL [Still breathless and agitated]
We were here—he slipped away from me somehow. He must have gone straight down to the House. I ran over, but when I got in under the Gallery he was speaking already. They expected something—I never heard it so still there. He gripped them from the first word—deadly—every syllable. It got some of those fellows. But all the time, under the silence you could feel a—sort of—of—current going round. And then Sherratt—I think it was—began it, and you saw the anger rising in them; but he kept them down—his quietness! The feeling! I've never seen anything like it there.

Then there was a whisper all over the House that fighting had begun. And the whole thing broke out— regular riot—as if they could have killed him. Some one tried to drag him down by the coat-tails, but he shook him off, and went on. Then he stopped dead and walked out, and the noise dropped like a stone.

The whole thing didn't last five minutes. It was fine, Mrs. More; like—like lava; he was the only cool person there. I wouldn't have missed it for anything—it was grand!

[**MORE** has appeared on the terrace, behind **STEEL**.

KATHERINE
Good-night, Mr. Steel.

STEEL [Startled]
Oh!—Good-night!

[He goes out into the hall. **KATHERINE** picks up **OLIVE'S** shoes, and stands clasping them to her breast. **MORE** comes in.

KATHERINE
You've cleared your conscience, then! I didn't think you'd hurt me so.

[**MORE** does not answer, still living in the scene he has gone through, and **KATHERINE** goes a little nearer to him.

KATHERINE
I'm with the country, heart and soul, Stephen. I warn you.

While they stand in silence, facing each other, the footman, **HENRY**, enters from the hall.

FOOTMAN
These notes, sir, from the House of Commons.

KATHERINE [Taking them]
You can have the room directly.

[The **FOOTMAN** goes out.

MORE
Open them!

[**KATHERINE** opens one after the other, and lets them fall on the table.

MORE
Well?

KATHERINE
What you might expect. Three of your best friends. It's begun.

MORE
'Ware Mob! [He gives a laugh] I must write to the Chief.

[**KATHERINE** makes an impulsive movement towards him; then quietly goes to the bureau, sits down and takes up a pen.

KATHERINE
Let me make the rough draft. [She waits] Yes?

MORE [Dictating]
"July 15th.

"DEAR SIR CHARLES, After my speech to-night, embodying my most unalterable convictions

[**KATHERINE** turns and looks up at him, but he is staring straight before him, and with a little movement of despair she goes on writing]

I have no alternative but to place the resignation of my Under-Secretaryship in your hands. My view, my faith in this matter may be wrong—but I am surely right to keep the flag of my faith flying. I imagine I need not enlarge on the reasons—"

THE CURTAIN FALLS.

ACT II

Before noon a few days later. The open windows of the dining-room let in the sunlight. On the table a number of newspapers are littered. **HELEN** is sitting there, staring straight before her. A newspaper boy runs by outside calling out his wares. At the sound she gets up anti goes out on to the terrace. **HUBERT** enters from the hall. He goes at once to the terrace, and draws **HELEN** into the room.

HELEN
Is it true—what they're shouting?

HUBERT
Yes. Worse than we thought. They got our men all crumpled up in the Pass—guns helpless. Ghastly beginning.

HELEN
Oh, Hubert!

HUBERT
My dearest girl!

[**HELEN** puts her face up to his. He kisses her. Then she turns quickly into the bay window. The door from the hall has been opened, and the footman, **HENRY**, comes in, preceding **WREFORD** and his sweetheart.

HENRY
Just wait here, will you, while I let Mrs. More know. [Catching sight of **HUBERT**] Beg pardon, sir!

HUBERT
All right, Henry. [Off-hand] Ah! Wreford!

[The **FOOTMAN** withdraws.

So you've brought her round. That's good! My sister'll look after her—don't you worry! Got everything packed? Three o'clock sharp.

WREFORD [A broad faced soldier, dressed in khaki with a certain look of dry humour, now dimmed-speaking with a West Country burr]
That's right, zurr; all's ready.

[**HELEN** has come out of the window, and is quietly looking at **WREFORD** and the girl standing there so awkwardly.

HELEN [Quietly]
Take care of him, Wreford.

HUBERT
We'll take care of each other, won't we, Wreford?

HELEN
How long have you been engaged?

THE GIRL [A pretty, indeterminate young woman]
Six months.

[She sobs suddenly.]

HELEN
Ah! He'll soon be safe back.

WREFORD
I'll owe 'em for this. [In a lacy voice to her] Don't 'ee now! Don't 'ee!

HELEN
No! Don't cry, please!

[She stands struggling with her own lips, then goes out on to the terrace, **HUBERT** following. **WREFORD** and his girl remain where they were, strange and awkward, she muffling her sobs.

WREFORD
Don't 'ee go on like that, Nance; I'll 'ave to take you 'ome. That's silly, now we've a-come. I might be dead and buried by the fuss you're makin'. You've a-drove the lady away. See!

[She regains control of herself as the door is opened and **KATHERINE** appears, accompanied by **OLIVE**, who regards **WREFORD** with awe and curiosity, and by **NURSE**, whose eyes are red, but whose manner is composed.

KATHERINE
My brother told me; so glad you've brought her.

WREFORD
Ye—as, M'. She feels me goin', a bit.

KATHERINE
Yes, yes! Still, it's for the country, isn't it?

THE GIRL
That's what Wreford keeps tellin' me. He've got to go—so it's no use upsettin' 'im. And of course I keep tellin' him I shall be all right.

NURSE [Whose eyes never leave her son's face]
And so you will.

THE GIRL
Wreford thought it'd comfort him to know you were interested in me. 'E's so 'ot-headed I'm sure somethin'll come to 'im.

KATHERINE
We've all got some one going. Are you coming to the docks? We must send them off in good spirits, you know.

OLIVE
Perhaps he'll get a medal.

KATHERINE
Olive!

NURSE
You wouldn't like for him to be hanging back, one of them anti-patriot, stop-the-war ones.

KATHERINE [Quickly]
Let me see—I have your address.

[Holding out her hand to **WREFORD**.

We'll look after her.

OLIVE [In a loud whisper]
Shall I lend him my toffee?

KATHERINE

If you like, dear. [To **WREFORD**] Now take care of my brother and yourself, and we'll take care of her.

WREFORD
Ye—as, M'.

[He then looks rather wretchedly at his girl, as if the interview had not done so much for him as he had hoped. She drops a little curtsey. **WREFORD** salutes.

OLIVE [Who has taken from the bureau a packet, places it in his hand]
It's very nourishing!

WREFORD
Thank you, miss.

[Then, nudging each other, and entangled in their feelings and the conventions, they pass out, shepherded by **NURSE**.

KATHERINE
Poor things!

OLIVE
What is an anti-patriot, stop-the-war one, Mummy?

KATHERINE [Taking up a newspaper]
Just a stupid name, dear—don't chatter!

OLIVE
But tell me just one weeny thing!

KATHERINE
Well?

OLIVE
Is Daddy one?

KATHERINE
Olive! How much do you know about this war?

OLIVE
They won't obey us properly. So we have to beat them, and take away their country. We shall, shan't we?

KATHERINE
Yes. But Daddy doesn't want us to; he doesn't think it fair, and he's been saying so. People are very angry with him.

OLIVE
Why isn't it fair? I suppose we're littler than them.

KATHERINE

No.

OLIVE

Oh! in history we always are. And we always win. That's why I like history. Which are you for, Mummy—us or them?

KATHERINE

Us.

OLIVE

Then I shall have to be. It's a pity we're not on the same side as Daddy. [**KATHERINE** shudders] Will they hurt him for not taking our side?

KATHERINE

I expect they will, Olive.

OLIVE

Then we shall have to be extra nice to him.

KATHERINE

If we can.

OLIVE

I can; I feel like it.

[**HELEN** and **HUBERT** have returned along the terrace. Seeing **KATHERINE** and the child, **HELEN** passes on, but **HUBERT** comes in at the French window.

OLIVE [Catching sight of him-softly]
Is Uncle Hubert going to the front to-day?

[**KATHERINE** nods.

But not grandfather?

KATHERINE

No, dear.

OLIVE

That's lucky for them, isn't it?

[**HUBERT** comes in. The presence of the child give him self-control.

HUBERT

Well, old girl, it's good-bye. [To **OLIVE**] What shall I bring you back, chick?

OLIVE
Are there shops at the front? I thought it was dangerous.

HUBERT
Not a bit.

OLIVE [Disillusioned]
Oh!

KATHERINE
Now, darling, give Uncle a good hug.

[Under cover of **OLIVE's** hug, **KATHERINE** repairs her courage.

KATHERINE
The Dad and I'll be with you all in spirit. Good-bye, old boy!

[They do not dare to kiss, and **HUBERT** goes out very stiff and straight, in the doorway passing **STEEL**, of whom he takes no notice. **STEEL** hesitates, and would go away.

KATHERINE
Come in, Mr. Steel.

STEEL
The deputation from Toulmin ought to be here, Mrs. More. It's twelve.

OLIVE [Having made a little ball of newspaper-slyly]
Mr. Steel, catch!

[She throws, and **STEEL** catches it in silence.

KATHERINE
Go upstairs, won't you, darling?

OLIVE
Mayn't I read in the window, Mummy? Then I shall see if any soldiers pass.

KATHERINE
No. You can go out on the terrace a little, and then you must go up.

[**OLIVE** goes reluctantly out on to the terrace.

STEEL
Awful news this morning of that Pass! And have you seen these? [Reading from the newspaper] "We will have no truck with the jargon of the degenerate who vilifies his country at such a moment. The Member for Toulmin has earned for himself the contempt of all virile patriots." [He takes up a second journal] "There is a certain type of public man who, even at his own expense, cannot resist the itch to

advertise himself. We would, at moments of national crisis, muzzle such persons, as we muzzle dogs that we suspect of incipient rabies...." They're in full cry after him!

KATHERINE
I mind much more all the creatures who are always flinging mud at the country making him their hero suddenly! You know what's in his mind?

STEEL
Oh! We must get him to give up that idea of lecturing everywhere against the war, Mrs. More; we simply must.

KATHERINE [Listening]
The deputation's come. Go and fetch him, Mr. Steel. He'll be in his room, at the House.

[**STEEL** goes out, and **KATHERINE** Stands at bay. In a moment he opens the door again, to usher in the deputation; then retires. The four gentlemen have entered as if conscious of grave issues. The first and most picturesque is **JAMES HOME**, a thin, tall, grey-bearded man, with plentiful hair, contradictious eyebrows, and the half-shy, half-bold manners, alternately rude and over polite, of one not accustomed to Society, yet secretly much taken with himself. He is dressed in rough tweeds, with a red silk tie slung through a ring, and is closely followed by **MARK WACE**, a waxy, round-faced man of middle-age, with sleek dark hair, traces of whisker, and a smooth way of continually rubbing his hands together, as if selling something to an esteemed customer. He is rather stout, wears dark clothes, with a large gold chain. Following him comes **CHARLES SHELDER**, a lawyer of fifty, with a bald egg-shaped head, and gold pince-nez. He has little side whiskers, a leathery, yellowish skin, a rather kind but watchful and dubious face, and when he speaks seems to have a plum in his mouth, which arises from the preponderance of his shaven upper lip. Last of the deputation comes **WILLIAM BANNING**, an energetic-looking, square-shouldered, self-made country-man, between fifty and sixty, with grey moustaches, ruddy face, and lively brown eyes.]

KATHERINE
How do you do, Mr. Home?

HOME [Bowing rather extravagantly over her hand, as if to show his independence of women's influence]
Mrs. More! We hardly expected—This is an honour.

WACE
How do you do, Ma'am?

KATHERINE
And you, Mr. Wace?

WACE
Thank you, Ma'am, well indeed!

SHELDER
How d'you do, Mrs. More?

KATHERINE
Very well, thank you, Mr. Shelder.

BANNING [Speaking with a rather broad country accent]
This is but a poor occasion, Ma'am.

KATHERINE
Yes, Mr. Banning. Do sit down, gentlemen.

[Seeing that they will not settle down while she is standing, she sits at the table. They gradually take their seats. Each member of the deputation in his own way is severely hanging back from any mention of the subject in hand; and **KATHERINE** as intent on drawing them to it.

KATHERINE
My husband will be here in two minutes. He's only over at the House.

SHELDER [Who is of higher standing and education than the others]
Charming position—this, Mrs. More! So near the—er—Centre of—Gravity um?

KATHERINE
I read the account of your second meeting at Toulmin.

BANNING
It's bad, Mrs. More—bad. There's no disguising it. That speech was moon-summer madness—Ah! it was! Take a lot of explaining away. Why did you let him, now? Why did you? Not your views, I'm sure!

[He looks at her, but for answer she only compresses her lips.

BANNING
I tell you what hit me—what's hit the whole constituency—and that's his knowing we were over the frontier, fighting already, when he made it.

KATHERINE
What difference does it make if he did know?

HOME
Hitting below the belt—I should have thought—you'll pardon me!

BANNING
Till war's begun, Mrs. More, you're entitled to say what you like, no doubt—but after! That's going against your country. Ah! his speech was strong, you know—his speech was strong.

KATHERINE
He had made up his mind to speak. It was just an accident the news coming then.

[A silence.

BANNING

Well, that's true, I suppose. What we really want is to make sure he won't break out again.

HOME
Very high-minded, his views of course—but, some consideration for the common herd. You'll pardon me!

SHELDER
We've come with the friendliest feelings, Mrs. More—but, you know, it won't do, this sort of thing!

WACE
We shall be able to smooth him down. Oh! surely.

BANNING
We'd be best perhaps not to mention about his knowing that fighting had begun.

[As he speaks, **MORE** enters through the French windows. They all rise.

MORE
Good-morning, gentlemen.

[He comes down to the table, but does not offer to shake hands.

BANNING
Well, Mr. More? You've made a woeful mistake, sir; I tell you to your face.

MORE
As everybody else does, Banning. Sit down again, please.

[They gradually resume their seats, and **MORE** sits in **KATHERINE's** chair. She alone remains standing leaning against the corner of the bay window, watching their faces.

BANNING
You've seen the morning's telegrams? I tell you, Mr. More—another reverse like that, and the flood will sweep you clean away. And I'll not blame it. It's only flesh and blood.

MORE
Allow for the flesh and blood in me, too, please. When I spoke the other night it was not without a certain feeling here.

[He touches his heart.

BANNING
But your attitude's so sudden—you'd not been going that length when you were down with us in May.

MORE
Do me the justice to remember that even then I was against our policy. It cost me three weeks' hard struggle to make up my mind to that speech. One comes slowly to these things, Banning.

SHELDER
Case of conscience?

MORE
Such things have happened, Shelder, even in politics.

SHELDER
You see, our ideals are naturally low—how different from yours!

[**MORE** smiles.

[**KATHERINE**, who has drawn near her husband, moves back again, as if relieved at this gleam of geniality. **WACE** rubs his hands.

BANNING
There's one thing you forget, sir. We send you to Parliament, representing us; but you couldn't find six men in the whole constituency that would have bidden you to make that speech.

MORE
I'm sorry; but I can't help my convictions, Banning.

SHELDER
What was it the prophet was without in his own country?

BANNING
Ah! but we're not funning, Mr. More. I've never known feeling run so high. The sentiment of both meetings was dead against you. We've had showers of letters to headquarters. Some from very good men—very warm friends of yours.

SHELDER
Come now! It's not too late. Let's go back and tell them you won't do it again.

MORE
Muzzling order?

BANNING [Bluntly]
That's about it.

MORE
Give up my principles to save my Parliamentary skin. Then, indeed, they might call me a degenerate!

[He touches the newspapers on the table.

[**KATHERINE** makes an abrupt and painful movement, then remains as still as before, leaning against the corner of the window-seat.

BANNING

Well, Well! I know. But we don't ask you to take your words back—we only want discretion in the future.

MORE

Conspiracy of silence! And have it said that a mob of newspapers have hounded me to it.

BANNING

They won't say that of you.

SHELDER

My dear More, aren't you rather dropping to our level? With your principles you ought not to care two straws what people say.

MORE

But I do. I can't betray the dignity and courage of public men. If popular opinion is to control the utterances of her politicians, then good-bye indeed to this country!

BANNING

Come now! I won't say that your views weren't sound enough before the fighting began. I've never liked our policy out there. But our blood's being spilled; and that makes all the difference. I don't suppose they'd want me exactly, but I'd be ready to go myself. We'd all of us be ready. And we can't have the man that represents us talking wild, until we've licked these fellows. That's it in a nutshell.

MORE

I understand your feeling, Banning. I tender you my resignation. I can't and won't hold on where I'm not wanted.

BANNING

No, no, no! Don't do that! [His accent broader and broader] You've 'ad your say, and there it is. Coom now! You've been our Member nine years, in rain and shine.

SHELDER

We want to keep you, More. Come! Give us your promise—that's a good man!

MORE

I don't make cheap promises. You ask too much.

[There is silence, and they all look at **MORE**.

SHELDER

There are very excellent reasons for the Government's policy.

MORE

There are always excellent reasons for having your way with the weak.

SHELDER

My dear More, how can you get up any enthusiasm for those cattle-lifting ruffians?

MORE
Better lift cattle than lift freedom.

SHELDER
Well, all we'll ask is that you shouldn't go about the country, saying so.

MORE
But that is just what I must do.

[Again they all look at **MORE** in consternation.

HOME
Not down our way, you'll pardon me.

WACE
Really—really, sir—

SHELDER
The time of crusades is past, More.

MORE
Is it?

BANNING
Ah! no, but we don't want to part with you, Mr. More. It's a bitter thing, this, after three elections. Look at the 'uman side of it! To speak ill of your country when there's been a disaster like this terrible business in the Pass. There's your own wife. I see her brother's regiment's to start this very afternoon. Come now—how must she feel?

[**MORE** breaks away to the bay window. The **DEPUTATION** exchange glances.

MORE [Turning]
To try to muzzle me like this—is going too far.

BANNING
We just want to put you out of temptation.

MORE
I've held my seat with you in all weathers for nine years. You've all been bricks to me. My heart's in my work, Banning; I'm not eager to undergo political eclipse at forty.

SHELDER
Just so—we don't want to see you in that quandary.

BANNING
It'd be no friendliness to give you a wrong impression of the state of feeling. Silence—till the bitterness is overpast; there's naught else for it, Mr. More, while you feel as you do. That tongue of yours! Come! You owe us something. You're a big man; it's the big view you ought to take.

MORE
I am trying to.

HOME
And what precisely is your view—you'll pardon my asking?

MORE [Turning on him]
Mr. Home a great country such as ours—is trustee for the highest sentiments of mankind. Do these few outrages justify us in stealing the freedom of this little people?

BANNING
Steal—their freedom! That's rather running before the hounds.

MORE
Ah, Banning! now we come to it. In your hearts you're none of you for that—neither by force nor fraud. And yet you all know that we've gone in there to stay, as we've gone into other lands—as all we big Powers go into other lands, when they're little and weak. The Prime Minister's words the other night were these: "If we are forced to spend this blood and money now, we must never again be forced." What does that mean but swallowing this country?

SHELDER
Well, and quite frankly, it'd be no bad thing.

HOME
We don't want their wretched country—we're forced.

MORE
We are not forced.

SHELDER
My dear More, what is civilization but the logical, inevitable swallowing up of the lower by the higher types of man? And what else will it be here?

MORE
We shall not agree there, Shelder; and we might argue it all day. But the point is, not whether you or I are right—the point is: What is a man who holds a faith with all his heart to do? Please tell me.

[There is a silence.]

BANNING [Simply]
I was just thinkin' of those poor fellows in the Pass.

MORE
I can see them, as well as you, Banning. But, imagine! Up in our own country—the Black Valley—twelve hundred foreign devils dead and dying—the crows busy over them—in our own country, our own valley—ours—ours—violated. Would you care about "the poor fellows" in that Pass?—Invading, stealing dogs! Kill them—kill them! You would, and I would, too!

[The passion of those words touches and grips as no arguments could; and they are silent.]

MORE
Well! What's the difference out there? I'm not so inhuman as not to want to see this disaster in the Pass wiped out. But once that's done, in spite of my affection for you; my ambitions, and they're not few; [Very low] in spite of my own wife's feeling, I must be free to raise my voice against this war.

BANNING [Speaking slowly, consulting the others, as it were, with his eyes]
Mr. More, there's no man I respect more than yourself. I can't tell what they'll say down there when we go back; but I, for one, don't feel it in me to take a hand in pressing you farther against your faith.

SHELDER
We don't deny that—that you have a case of sorts.

WACE
No—surely.

SHELDER
A—man should be free, I suppose, to hold his own opinions.

MORE
Thank you, Shelder.

BANNING
Well! well! We must take you as you are; but it's a rare pity; there'll be a lot of trouble—

[His eyes light on Honk who is leaning forward with hand raised to his ear, listening. Very faint, from far in the distance, there is heard a skirling sound. All become conscious of it, all listen.]

HOME [Suddenly]
Bagpipes!

[The figure of **OLIVE** flies past the window, out on the terrace. **KATHERINE** turns, as if to follow her.]

SHELDER
Highlanders!

[He rises. **KATHERINE** goes quickly out on to the terrace. One by one they all follow to the window. One by one go out on to the terrace, till **MORE** is left alone. He turns to the bay window. The music is swelling, coming nearer. **MORE** leaves the window—his face distorted by the strafe of his emotions. He paces the room, taking, in some sort, the rhythm of the march.

[Slowly the music dies away in the distance to a drum-tap and the tramp of a company. **MORE** stops at the table, covering his eyes with his hands.

[The **DEPUTATION** troop back across the terrace, and come in at the French windows. Their faces and manners have quite changed. **KATHERINE** follows them as far as the window.

HOME [In a strange, almost threatening voice]
It won't do, Mr. More. Give us your word, to hold your peace!

SHELDER
Come! More.

WACE
Yes, indeed—indeed!

BANNING
We must have it.

MORE [Without lifting his head]
I—I—

The drum-tap of a regiment marching is heard.

BANNING
Can you hear that go by, man—when your country's just been struck?

[Now comes the scale and mutter of a following **CROWD**.

MORE
I give you—

[Then, sharp and clear above all other sounds, the words: "Give the beggars hell, boys!" "Wipe your feet
on their dirty country!" "Don't leave 'em a gory acre!" And a burst of hoarse cheering.

MORE [Flinging up his head]
That's reality! By Heaven! No!

KATHERINE
Oh!

SHELDER
In that case, we'll go.

BANNING
You mean it? You lose us, then!

[**MORE** bows.

HOME
Good riddance! [Venomously—his eyes darting between **MORE** and **KATHERINE**] Go and stump the
country! Find out what they think of you! You'll pardon me!

[One by one, without a word, only **BANNING** looking back, they pass out into the hall. **MORE** sits down at the table before the pile of newspapers. **KATHERINE**, in the window, never moves. **OLIVE** comes along the terrace to her mother.

OLIVE
They were nice ones! Such a lot of dirty people following, and some quite clean, Mummy. [Conscious from her mother's face that something is very wrong, she looks at her father, and then steals up to his side] Uncle Hubert's gone, Daddy; and Auntie Helen's crying. And—look at Mummy!

[**MORE** raises his head and looks.

OLIVE
Do be on our side! Do!

[She rubs her cheek against his. Feeling that he does not rub his cheek against hers, **OLIVE** stands away, and looks from him to her mother in wonder.

THE CURTAIN FALLS

ACT III

SCENE I

A cobble-stoned alley, without pavement, behind a suburban theatre. The tall, blind, dingy-yellowish wall of the building is plastered with the tattered remnants of old entertainment bills, and the words: "To Let," and with several torn, and one still virgin placard, containing this announcement: "Stop-the-War Meeting, October 1st. Addresses by STEPHEN MORE, Esq., and others." The alley is plentifully strewn with refuse and scraps of paper. Three stone steps, inset, lead to the stage door. It is a dark night, and a street lamp close to the wall throws all the light there is. A faint, confused murmur, as of distant hooting is heard. Suddenly a boy comes running, then two rough girls hurry past in the direction of the sound; and the alley is again deserted. The stage door opens, and a doorkeeper, poking his head out, looks up and down. He withdraws, but in a second reappears, preceding three black-coated gentlemen.

DOORKEEPER
It's all clear. You can get away down here, gentlemen. Keep to the left, then sharp to the right, round the corner.

THE THREE [Dusting themselves, and settling their ties]
Thanks, very much! Thanks!

FIRST BLACK-COATED GENTLEMAN
Where's More? Isn't he coming?

[They are joined by a fourth black-coated **GENTLEMAN**.

FOURTH BLACK-COATED GENTLEMAN
Just behind. [To the **DOORKEEPER**] Thanks.

[They hurry away. The **DOORKEEPER** retires. Another boy runs past. Then the door opens again. **STEEL** and **MORE** come out.

[**MORE** stands hesitating on the steps; then turns as if to go back.

STEEL
Come along, sir, come!

MORE
It sticks in my gizzard, Steel.

STEEL [Running his arm through **MORE'S**, and almost dragging him down the steps]
You owe it to the theatre people.

[**MORE** still hesitates.

We might be penned in there another hour; you told Mrs. More half-past ten; it'll only make her anxious. And she hasn't seen you for six weeks.

MORE
All right; don't dislocate my arm.

[They move down the steps, and away to the left, as a boy comes running down the alley. Sighting **MORE**, he stops dead, spins round, and crying shrilly: "'Ere 'e is! That's 'im! 'Ere 'e is!" he bolts back in the direction whence he came.

STEEL
Quick, Sir, quick!

MORE
That is the end of the limit, as the foreign ambassador remarked.

STEEL [Pulling him back towards the door]
Well! come inside again, anyway!

[A number of **MEN** and **BOYS**, and a few young **GIRLS**, are trooping quickly from the left. A motley crew, out for excitement; loafers, artisans, navvies; girls, rough or dubious. All in the mood of hunters, and having tasted blood. They gather round the steps displaying the momentary irresolution and curiosity that follows on a new development of any chase. **MORE**, on the bottom step, turns and eyes them.

A GIRL [At the edge]
Which is 'im! The old 'un or the young?

[**MORE** turns, and mounts the remaining steps.

TALL YOUTH [With lank black hair under a bowler hat]
You blasted traitor!

[**MORE** faces round at the volley of jeering that follows; the chorus of booing swells, then gradually dies, as if they realized that they were spoiling their own sport.

A ROUGH GIRL
Don't frighten the poor feller!

[**A GIRL** beside her utters a shrill laugh.]

STEEL [Tugging at **MORE's** arm]
Come along, sir.

MORE [Shaking his arm free—to the crowd]
Well, what do you want?

A VOICE
Speech.

MORE
Indeed! That's new.

ROUGH VOICE [At the back of the crowd]
Look at his white liver. You can see it in his face.

A BIG NAVY [In front] Shut it! Give 'im a chanst!

TALL YOUTH
Silence for the blasted traitor?

[**A YOUTH** plays the concertina; there is laughter, then an abrupt silence.

MORE
You shall have it in a nutshell!

A SHOPBOY [Flinging a walnut-shell which strikes **MORE** on the shoulder]
Here y'are!

MORE
Go home, and think! If foreigners invaded us, wouldn't you be fighting tooth and nail like those tribesmen, out there?

TALL YOUTH
Treacherous dogs! Why don't they come out in the open?

MORE
They fight the best way they can.

[A burst of hooting is led by a soldier in khaki on the outskirt.

MORE
My friend there in khaki led that hooting. I've never said a word against our soldiers. It's the Government I condemn for putting them to this, and the Press for hounding on the Government, and all of you for being led by the nose to do what none of you would do, left to yourselves.

[The **TALL YOUTH** leads a somewhat unspontaneous burst of execration.

MORE
I say not one of you would go for a weaker man.

VOICES IN THE CROWD.

ROUGH VOICE
Tork sense!

GIRL'S VOICE
He's gittin' at you!

TALL YOUTH'S VOICE
Shiny skunk!

A NAVVY [Suddenly shouldering forward]
Look 'ere, Mister! Don't you come gaflin' to those who've got mates out there, or it'll be the worse for you-you go 'ome!

COCKNEY VOICE
And git your wife to put cottonwool in yer ears.

[A spurt of laughter.

A FRIENDLY VOICE [From the outskirts]
Shame! there! Bravo, More! Keep it up!

[A scuffle drowns this cry.

MORE [With vehemence]
Stop that! Stop that! You—!

TALL YOUTH
Traitor!

AN ARTISAN
Who black-legged?

MIDDLE-AGED MAN

Ought to be shot-backin' his country's enemies!

MORE
Those tribesmen are defending their homes.

TWO VOICES
Hear! hear!

[They are hustled into silence.]

TALL YOUTH
Wind-bag!

MORE [With sudden passion]
Defending their homes! Not mobbing unarmed men!

[**STEEL** again pulls at his arm.

ROUGH VOICE
Shut it, or we'll do you in!

MORE [Recovering his coolness]
Ah! Do me in by all means! You'd deal such a blow at cowardly mobs as wouldn't be forgotten in your time.

STEEL
For God's sake, sir!

MORE [Shaking off his touch]
Well!

[There is an ugly rush, checked by the fall of the foremost figures, thrown too suddenly against the bottom step. The crowd recoils.

[There is a momentary lull, and **MORE** stares steadily down at them.

COCKNEY VOICE
Don't 'e speak well! What eloquence!

[Two or three nutshells and a piece of orange-peel strike **MORE** across the face. He takes no notice.

ROUGH VOICE
That's it! Give 'im some encouragement.

The jeering laughter is changed to anger by the contemptuous smile on **MORE'S** face.

A TALL YOUTH
Traitor!

A VOICE
Don't stand there like a stuck pig.

A ROUGH
Let's 'ave 'im dahn off that!

[Under cover of the applause that greets this, he strikes **MORE** across the legs with a belt. **STEEL** starts forward. **MORE**, flinging out his arm, turns him back, and resumes his tranquil staring at the crowd, in whom the sense of being foiled by this silence is fast turning to rage.

THE CROWD
Speak up, or get down! Get off! Get away, there—or we'll make you! Go on!

[**MORE** remains immovable.

A YOUTH [In a lull of disconcertion]
I'll make 'im speak! See!

[He darts forward and spits, defiling **MORES** hand. **MORE** jerks it up as if it had been stung, then stands as still as ever. A spurt of laughter dies into a shiver of repugnance at the action. The shame is fanned again to fury by the sight of **MORES** scornful face.

TALL YOUTH [Out of murmuring]
Shift! or you'll get it!

A VOICE
Enough of your ugly mug!

A ROUGH
Give 'im one!

[Two flung stones strike **MORE.** He staggers and nearly falls, then rights himself.

A GIRL'S VOICE
Shame!

FRIENDLY VOICE
Bravo, More! Stick to it!

A ROUGH
Give 'im another!

A VOICE
No!

A GIRL'S VOICE
Let 'im alone! Come on, Billy, this ain't no fun!

[Still looking up at **MORE**, the whole crowd falls into an uneasy silence, broken only by the shuffling of feet. Then the **BIG NAVVY** in the front rank turns and elbows his way out to the edge of the crowd.

THE NAVVY
Let 'im be!

[With half-sullen and half-shamefaced acquiescence the crowd breaks up and drifts back whence it came, till the alley is nearly empty.

MORE [As if coming to, out of a trance-wiping his hand and dusting his coat]
Well, Steel!

[And followed by **STEEL**, he descends the steps and moves away. Two **POLICEMEN** pass glancing up at the broken glass. One of them stops and makes a note.

THE CURTAIN FALLS.

SCENE II

The window-end of Katherine's bedroom, panelled in cream-coloured wood. The light from four candles is falling on **KATHERINE**, who is sitting before the silver mirror of an old oak dressing-table, brushing her hair. A door, on the left, stands ajar. An oak chair against the wall close to a recessed window is all the other furniture. Through this window the blue night is seen, where a mist is rolled out flat amongst trees, so that only dark clumps of boughs show here and there, beneath a moonlit sky. As the curtain rises, **KATHERINE**, with brush arrested, is listening. She begins again brushing her hair, then stops, and taking a packet of letters from a drawer of her dressing-table, reads. Through the just open door behind her comes the voice of **OLIVE**.

OLIVE
Mummy! I'm awake!

[But **KATHERINE** goes on reading; and **OLIVE** steals into the room in her nightgown.

OLIVE [At **KATHERINE'S** elbow—examining her watch on its stand]
It's fourteen minutes to eleven.

KATHERINE
Olive, Olive!

OLIVE
I just wanted to see the time. I never can go to sleep if I try—it's quite helpless, you know. Is there a victory yet?

[**KATHERINE**, shakes her head.

Oh! I prayed extra special for one in the evening papers. [Straying round her mother] Hasn't Daddy come?

KATHERINE
Not yet.

OLIVE
Are you waiting for him?

[Burying her face in her mother's hair.

Your hair is nice, Mummy. It's particular to-night.

[**KATHERINE** lets fall her brush, and looks at her almost in alarm.

OLIVE
How long has Daddy been away?

KATHERINE
Six weeks.

OLIVE
It seems about a hundred years, doesn't it? Has he been making speeches all the time?

KATHERINE
Yes.

OLIVE
To-night, too?

KATHERINE
Yes.

OLIVE
The night that man was here whose head's too bald for anything—oh! Mummy, you know—the one who cleans his teeth so termendously—I heard Daddy making a speech to the wind. It broke a wine-glass. His speeches must be good ones, mustn't they!

KATHERINE
Very.

OLIVE
It felt funny; you couldn't see any wind, you know.

KATHERINE
Talking to the wind is an expression, Olive.

OLIVE

Does Daddy often?

KATHERINE
Yes, nowadays.

OLIVE
What does it mean?

KATHERINE
Speaking to people who won't listen.

OLIVE
What do they do, then?

KATHERINE
Just a few people go to hear him, and then a great crowd comes and breaks in; or they wait for him outside, and throw things, and hoot.

OLIVE
Poor Daddy! Is it people on our side who throw things?

KATHERINE
Yes, but only rough people.

OLIVE
Why does he go on doing it? I shouldn't.

KATHERINE
He thinks it is his duty.

OLIVE
To your neighbour, or only to God?

KATHERINE
To both.

OLIVE
Oh! Are those his letters?

KATHERINE
Yes.

OLIVE [Reading from the letter]
"My dear Heart." Does he always call you his dear heart, Mummy? It's rather jolly, isn't it? "I shall be home about half-past ten to-morrow night. For a few hours the fires of p-u-r-g-a-t-or-y will cease to burn—" What are the fires of p-u-r-g-a-t-o-r-y?

KATHERINE [Putting away the letters]

Come, Olive!

OLIVE
But what are they?

KATHERINE
Daddy means that he's been very unhappy.

OLIVE
Have you, too?

KATHERINE
Yes.

OLIVE [Cheerfully]
So have I. May I open the window?

KATHERINE
No; you'll let the mist in.

OLIVE
Isn't it a funny mist-all flat!

KATHERINE
Now, come along, frog!

OLIVE [Making time]
Mummy, when is Uncle Hubert coming back?

KATHERINE
We don't know, dear.

OLIVE
I suppose Auntie Helen'll stay with us till he does.

KATHERINE
Yes.

OLIVE
That's something, isn't it?

KATHERINE [Picking her up]
Now then!

OLIVE [Deliciously limp]
Had I better put in the duty to your neighbour if there isn't a victory soon?

[As they pass through the door.

You're tickling under my knee!

[Little gurgles of pleasure follow. Then silence. Then a drowsy voice.

I must keep awake for Daddy.

[KATHERINE comes back. She is about to leave the door a little open, when she hears a knock on the other door. It is opened a few inches, and NURSE'S voice says: "Can I come in, Ma'am?" The NURSE comes in.

KATHERINE [Shutting OLIVE's door, and going up to her]
What is it, Nurse?

NURSE [Speaking in a low voice]
I've been meaning to—I'll never do it in the daytime. I'm giving you notice.

KATHERINE
Nurse! You too!

[She looks towards OLIVE'S room with dismay. The NURSE smudges a slow tear away from her cheek.

NURSE
I want to go right away at once.

KATHERINE
Leave Olive! That is the sins of the fathers with a vengeance.

NURSE
I've had another letter from my son. No, Miss Katherine, while the master goes on upholdin' these murderin' outlandish creatures, I can't live in this house, not now he's coming back.

KATHERINE
But, Nurse—!

NURSE
It's not like them [With an ineffable gesture] downstairs, because I'm frightened of the mob, or of the window's bein' broke again, or mind what the boys in the street say. I should think not—no! It's my heart. I'm sore night and day thinkin' of my son, and him lying out there at night without a rag of dry clothing, and water that the bullocks won't drink, and maggots in the meat; and every day one of his friends laid out stark and cold, and one day—'imself perhaps. If anything were to 'appen to him. I'd never forgive meself—here. Ah! Miss Katherine, I wonder how you bear it—bad news comin' every day—And Sir John's face so sad—And all the time the master speaking against us, as it might be Jonah 'imself.

KATHERINE
But, Nurse, how can you leave us, you?

NURSE [Smudging at her cheeks]
There's that tells me it's encouragin' something to happen, if I stay here; and Mr. More coming back to-night. You can't serve God and Mammon, the Bible says.

KATHERINE
Don't you know what it's costing him?

NURSE
Ah! Cost him his seat, and his reputation; and more than that it'll cost him, to go against the country.

KATHERINE
He's following his conscience.

NURSE
And others must follow theirs, too. No, Miss Katherine, for you to let him—you, with your three brothers out there, and your father fair wasting away with grief. Sufferin' too as you've been these three months past. What'll you feel if anything happens to my three young gentlemen out there, to my dear Mr. Hubert that I nursed myself, when your precious mother couldn't? What would she have said—with you in the camp of his enemies?

KATHERINE
Nurse, Nurse!

NURSE
In my paper they say he's encouraging these heathens and makin' the foreigners talk about us; and every day longer the war lasts, there's our blood on this house.

KATHERINE [Turning away]
Nurse, I can't—I won't listen.

NURSE [Looking at her intently]
Ah! You'll move him to leave off! I see your heart, my dear. But if you don't, then go I must!

[She nods her head gravely, goes to the door of **OLIVE'S** room, opens it gently, stands looking for a-moment, then with the words "My Lamb!" she goes in noiselessly and closes the door.

[**KATHERINE** turns back to her glass, puts back her hair, and smooths her lips and eyes. The door from the corridor is opened, and **HELEN's** voice says: "Kit! You're not in bed?"

KATHERINE
No.

[**HELEN** too is in a wrapper, with a piece of lace thrown over her head. Her face is scared and miserable, and she runs into **KATHERINE's** arms.

KATHERINE
My dear, what is it?

HELEN
I've seen—a vision!

KATHERINE
Hssh! You'll wake Olive!

HELEN [Staring before her]
I'd just fallen asleep, and I saw a plain that seemed to run into the sky—like—that fog. And on it there were—dark things. One grew into a body without a head, and a gun by its side. And one was a man sitting huddled up, nursing a wounded leg. He had the face of Hubert's servant, Wreford. And then I saw—Hubert. His face was all dark and thin; and he had—a wound, an awful wound here

[She touches her breast.

The blood was running from it, and he kept trying to stop it—oh! Kit—by kissing it

[She pauses, stifled by emotion.

Then I heard Wreford laugh, and say vultures didn't touch live bodies. And there came a voice, from somewhere, calling out: "Oh! God! I'm dying!" And Wreford began to swear at it, and I heard Hubert say: "Don't, Wreford; let the poor fellow be!" But the voice went on and on, moaning and crying out: "I'll lie here all night dying—and then I'll die!" And Wreford dragged himself along the ground; his face all devilish, like a man who's going to kill.

KATHERINE
My dear! HOW ghastly!

HELEN
Still that voice went on, and I saw Wreford take up the dead man's gun. Then Hubert got upon his feet, and went tottering along, so feebly, so dreadfully—but before he could reach and stop him, Wreford fired at the man who was crying. And Hubert called out: "You brute!" and fell right down. And when Wreford saw him lying there, he began to moan and sob, but Hubert never stirred. Then it all got black again—and I could see a dark woman—thing creeping, first to the man without a head; then to Wreford; then to Hubert, and it touched him, and sprang away. And it cried out: "A-ai-ah!" [Pointing out at the mist] Look! Out there! The dark things!

KATHERINE [Putting her arms round her]
Yes, dear, yes! You must have been looking at the mist.

HELEN [Strangely calm]
He's dead!

KATHERINE
It was only a dream.

HELEN
You didn't hear that cry. [She listens] That's Stephen. Forgive me, Kit; I oughtn't to have upset you, but I couldn't help coming.

[She goes out, **KATHERINE**, into whom her emotion seems to have passed, turns feverishly to the window, throws it open and leans out. **MORE** comes in.

MORE
Kit!

Catching sight of her figure in the window, he goes quickly to her.

KATHERINE
Ah!

[She has mastered her emotion.

MORE
Let me look at you!

[He draws her from the window to the candle-light, and looks long at her.

MORE
What have you done to your hair?

KATHERINE
Nothing.

MORE
It's wonderful to-night.

[He takes it greedily and buries his face in it.

KATHERINE [Drawing her hair away]
Well?

MORE
At last!

KATHERINE [Pointing to **OLIVE's** room]
Hssh!

MORE
How is she?

KATHERINE
All right.

MORE
And you?

[**KATHERINE** shrugs her shoulders.

MORE
Six weeks!

KATHERINE
Why have you come?

MORE
Why!

KATHERINE
You begin again the day after tomorrow. Was it worth while?

MORE
Kit!

KATHERINE
It makes it harder for me, that's all.

MORE [Staring at her]
What's come to you?

KATHERINE
Six weeks is a long time to sit and read about your meetings.

MORE
Put that away to-night. [He touches her] This is what travellers feel when they come out of the desert to-water.

KATHERINE [Suddenly noticing the cut on his forehead]
Your forehead! It's cut.

MORE
It's nothing.

KATHERINE
Oh! Let me bathe it!

MORE
No, dear! It's all right.

KATHERINE [Turning away]
Helen has just been telling me a dream she's had of Hubert's death.

MORE
Poor child!

KATHERINE
Dream bad dreams, and wait, and hide oneself—there's been nothing else to do. Nothing, Stephen—nothing!

MORE
Hide? Because of me?

[**KATHERINE** nods.

MORE [With a movement of distress]
I see. I thought from your letters you were coming to feel—. Kit! You look so lovely!

[Suddenly he sees that she is crying, and goes quickly to her.

MORE
My dear, don't cry! God knows I don't want to make things worse for you. I'll go away.

[She draws away from him a little, and after looking long at her, he sits down at the dressing-table and begins turning over the brushes and articles of toilet, trying to find words.

MORE
Never look forward. After the time I've had—I thought—tonight—it would be summer—I thought it would be you—and everything!

[While he is speaking **KATHERINE** has stolen closer. She suddenly drops on her knees by his side and wraps his hand in her hair. He turns and clasps her.

MORE
Kit!

KATHERINE
Ah! yes! But-to-morrow it begins again. Oh! Stephen! How long—how long am I to be torn in two?

[Drawing back in his arms.

I can't—can't bear it.

MORE
My darling!

KATHERINE
Give it up! For my sake! Give it up! [Pressing closer to him] It shall be me—and everything—

MORE
God!

KATHERINE
It shall be—if—if—

MORE [Aghast]
You're not making terms? Bargaining? For God's sake, Kit!

KATHERINE
For God's sake, Stephen!

MORE
You!—of all people—you!

KATHERINE
Stephen!

[For a moment **MORE** yields utterly, then shrinks back.

MORE
A bargain! It's selling my soul!

He struggles out of her arms, gets up, and stands without speaking, staring at her, and wiping the sweat from his forehead. **KATHERINE** remains some seconds on her knees, gazing up at him, not realizing. Then her head droops; she too gets up and stands apart, with her wrapper drawn close round her. It is as if a cold and deadly shame had come to them both. Quite suddenly **MORE** turns, and, without looking back, feebly makes his way out of the room. When he is gone **KATHERINE** drops on her knees and remains there motionless, huddled in her hair.

THE CURTAIN FALLS

ACT IV

It is between lights, the following day, in the dining-room of More's house. The windows are closed, but curtains are not drawn. **STEEL** is seated at the bureau, writing a letter from **MORE's** dictation.

STEEL [Reading over the letter]
"No doubt we shall have trouble. But, if the town authorities at the last minute forbid the use of the hall, we'll hold the meeting in the open. Let bills be got out, and an audience will collect in any case."

MORE
They will.

STEEL
"Yours truly"; I've signed for you.

[**MORE** nods.

STEEL [Blotting and enveloping the letter]
You know the servants have all given notice—except Henry.

MORE
Poor Henry!

STEEL
It's partly nerves, of course—the windows have been broken twice—but it's partly—

MORE
Patriotism. Quite! they'll do the next smashing themselves. That reminds me—to-morrow you begin holiday, Steel.

STEEL
Oh, no!

MORE
My dear fellow—yes. Last night ended your sulphur cure. Truly sorry ever to have let you in for it.

STEEL
Some one must do the work. You're half dead as it is.

MORE
There's lots of kick in me.

STEEL
Give it up, sir. The odds are too great. It isn't worth it.

MORE
To fight to a finish; knowing you must be beaten—is anything better worth it?

STEEL
Well, then, I'm not going.

MORE
This is my private hell, Steel; you don't roast in it any longer. Believe me, it's a great comfort to hurt no one but yourself.

STEEL
I can't leave you, sir.

MORE
My dear boy, you're a brick—but we've got off by a miracle so far, and I can't have the responsibility of you any longer. Hand me over that correspondence about to-morrow's meeting.

[**STEEL** takes some papers from his pocket, but does not hand them.

MORE
Come!

[He stretches out his hand for the papers. As **STEEL** still draws back, he says more sharply.

Give them to me, Steel!

[**STEEL** hands them over]

Now, that ends it, d'you see?

[They stand looking at each other; then **STEEL**, very much upset, turns and goes out of the room. **MORE**, who has watched him with a sorry smile, puts the papers into a dispatch-case. As he is closing the bureau, the footman **HENRY** enters, announcing: "Mr. Mendip, sir." **MENDIP** comes in, and the **FOOTMAN** withdraws. **MORE** turns to his visitor, but does not hold out his hand.

MENDIP [Taking **MORE'S** hand]
Give me credit for a little philosophy, my friend. Mrs. More told me you'd be back to-day. Have you heard?

MORE
What?

MENDIP
There's been a victory.

MORE
Thank God!

MENDIP
Ah! So you actually are flesh and blood.

MORE
Yes!

MENDIP
Take off the martyr's shirt, Stephen. You're only flouting human nature.

MORE
So—even you defend the mob!

MENDIP
My dear fellow, you're up against the strongest common instinct in the world. What do you expect? That the man in the street should be a Quixote? That his love of country should express itself in philosophic altruism? What on earth do you expect? Men are very simple creatures; and Mob is just conglomerate essence of simple men.

MORE
Conglomerate excrescence. Mud of street and market-place gathered in a torrent—This blind howling "patriotism"—what each man feels in here?

[He touches his breast.

No!

MENDIP
You think men go beyond instinct—they don't. All they know is that something's hurting that image of themselves that they call country. They just feel something big and religious, and go it blind.

MORE
This used to be the country of free speech. It used to be the country where a man was expected to hold to his faith.

MENDIP
There are limits to human nature, Stephen.

MORE
Let no man stand to his guns in face of popular attack. Still your advice, is it?

MENDIP
My advice is: Get out of town at once. The torrent you speak of will be let loose the moment this news is out. Come, my dear fellow, don't stay here!

MORE
Thanks! I'll see that Katherine and Olive go.

MENDIP
Go with them! If your cause is lost, that's no reason why you should be.

MORE
There's the comfort of not running away. And—I want comfort.

MENDIP
This is bad, Stephen; bad, foolish—foolish. Well! I'm going to the House. This way?

MORE
Down the steps, and through the gate. Good-bye?

[**KATHERINE** has come in followed by **NURSE**, hatted and cloaked, with a small bag in her hand. **KATHERINE** takes from the bureau a cheque which she hands to the **NURSE**. **MORE** comes in from the terrace.

MORE
You're wise to go, Nurse.

NURSE
You've treated my poor dear badly, sir. Where's your heart?

MORE

In full use.

NURSE

On those heathens. Don't your own hearth and home come first? Your wife, that was born in time of war, with her own father fighting, and her grandfather killed for his country. A bitter thing, to have the windows of her house broken, and be pointed at by the boys in the street.

[**MORE** stands silent under this attack, looking at his wife.

KATHERINE
Nurse!

NURSE

It's unnatural, sir—what you're doing! To think more of those savages than of your own wife! Look at her! Did you ever see her look like that? Take care, sir, before it's too late!

MORE
Enough, please!

[**NURSE** stands for a moment doubtful; looks long at **KATHERINE**; then goes.

MORE [Quietly]
There has been a victory.

[He goes out. **KATHERINE** is breathing fast, listening to the distant hum and stir rising in the street. She runs to the window as the footman, HENRY, entering, says: "Sir John Julian, Ma'am!" **SIR JOHN** comes in, a newspaper in his hand.]

KATHERINE
At last! A victory!

SIR JOHN
Thank God!

[He hands her the paper.

KATHERINE
Oh, Dad!

[She tears the paper open, and feverishly reads.

KATHERINE
At last!

[The distant hum in the street is rising steadily. But **SIR JOHN**, after the one exultant moment when he handed her the paper, stares dumbly at the floor.

KATHERINE [Suddenly conscious of his gravity]

Father!

SIR JOHN
There is other news.

KATHERINE
One of the boys? Hubert?

[**SIR JOHN** bows his head.

KATHERINE
Killed?

[**SIR JOHN** again bows his head.

KATHERINE
The dream! [She covers her face] Poor Helen!

[They stand for a few seconds silent, then **SIR JOHN** raises his head, and putting up a hand, touches her wet cheek.

SIR JOHN [Huskily]
Whom the gods love—

KATHERINE
Hubert!

SIR JOHN
And hulks like me go on living!

KATHERINE
Dear Dad!

SIR JOHN
But we shall drive the ruffians now! We shall break them. Stephen back?

KATHERINE
Last night.

SIR JOHN
Has he finished his blasphemous speech-making at last?

[**KATHERINE** shakes her head.

Not?

[Then, seeing that **KATHERINE** is quivering with emotion, he strokes her hand.

SIR JOHN
My dear! Death is in many houses!

KATHERINE
I must go to Helen. Tell Stephen, Father. I can't.

SIR JOHN
If you wish, child.

[She goes out, leaving **SIR JOHN** to his grave, puzzled grief, and in a few seconds **MORE** comes in.

MORE
Yes, Sir John. You wanted me?

SIR JOHN
Hubert is killed.

MORE
Hubert!

SIR JOHN
By these—whom you uphold. Katherine asked me to let you know. She's gone to Helen. I understand you only came back last night from your—No word I can use would give what I feel about that. I don't know how things stand now between you and Katherine; but I tell you this, Stephen: you've tried her these last two months beyond what any woman ought to bear!

[**MORE** makes a gesture of pain.

SIR JOHN
When you chose your course—

MORE
Chose!

SIR JOHN
You placed yourself in opposition to every feeling in her. You knew this might come. It may come again with another of my sons.

MORE
I would willingly change places with any one of them.

SIR JOHN
Yes—I can believe in your unhappiness. I cannot conceive of greater misery than to be arrayed against your country. If I could have Hubert back, I would not have him at such a price—no, nor all my sons. 'Pro patri mori'—My boy, at all events, is happy!

MORE
Yes!

SIR JOHN
Yet you can go on doing what you are! What devil of pride has got into you, Stephen?

MORE
Do you imagine I think myself better than the humblest private fighting out there? Not for a minute.

SIR JOHN
I don't understand you. I always thought you devoted to Katherine.

MORE
Sir John, you believe that country comes before wife and child?

SIR JOHN
I do.

MORE
So do I.

SIR JOHN [Bewildered]
Whatever my country does or leaves undone, I no more presume to judge her than I presume to judge my God. [With all the exaltation of the suffering he has undergone for her] My country!

MORE
I would give all I have—for that creed.

SIR JOHN [Puzzled]
Stephen, I've never looked on you as a crank; I always believed you sane and honest. But this is— visionary mania.

MORE
Vision of what might be.

SIR JOHN
Why can't you be content with what the grandest nation—the grandest men on earth—have found good enough for them? I've known them, I've seen what they could suffer, for our country.

MORE
Sir John, imagine what the last two months have been to me! To see people turn away in the street—old friends pass me as if I were a wall! To dread the post! To go to bed every night with the sound of hooting in my ears! To know that my name is never referred to without contempt—

SIR JOHN
You have your new friends. Plenty of them, I understand.

MORE
Does that make up for being spat at as I was last night? Your battles are fool's play to it.

[The stir and rustle of the crowd in the street grows louder. **SIR JOHN** turns his head towards it.

SIR JOHN
You've heard there's been a victory. Do you carry your unnatural feeling so far as to be sorry for that?

[**MORE** shakes his head.

That's something! For God's sake, Stephen, stop before it's gone past mending. Don't ruin your life with Katherine. Hubert was her favourite brother; you are backing those who killed him. Think what that means to her! Drop this—mad Quixotism—idealism—whatever you call it. Take Katherine away. Leave the country till the thing's over—this country of yours that you're opposing, and—and—traducing. Take her away! Come! What good are you doing? What earthly good? Come, my boy! Before you're utterly undone.

MORE
Sir John! Our men are dying out there for, the faith that's in them! I believe my faith the higher, the better for mankind—Am I to slink away? Since I began this campaign I've found hundreds who've thanked me for taking this stand. They look on me now as their leader. Am I to desert them? When you led your forlorn hope—did you ask yourself what good you were doing, or, whether you'd come through alive? It's my forlorn hope not to betray those who are following me; and not to help let die a fire—a fire that's sacred—not only now in this country, but in all countries, for all time.

SIR JOHN [After a long stare]
I give you credit for believing what you say. But let me tell you whatever that fire you talk of—I'm too old-fashioned to grasp—one fire you are letting die—your wife's love. By God! This crew of your new friends, this crew of cranks and jays, if they can make up to you for the loss of her love—of your career, of all those who used to like and respect you—so much the better for you. But if you find yourself bankrupt of affection—alone as the last man on earth; if this business ends in your utter ruin and destruction—as it must—I shall not pity—I cannot pity you. Good-night!

[He marches to the door, opens it, and goes out. **MORE** is left standing perfectly still. The stir and murmur of the street is growing all the time, and slowly forces itself on his consciousness. He goes to the bay window and looks out; then rings the bell. It is not answered, and, after turning up the lights, he rings again. **KATHERINE** comes in. She is wearing a black hat, and black outdoor coat. She speaks coldly without looking up.

KATHERINE
You rang!

MORE
For them to shut this room up.

KATHERINE
The servants have gone out. They're afraid of the house being set on fire.

MORE
I see.

KATHERINE
They have not your ideals to sustain them.

[**MORE** winces.

I am going with Helen and Olive to Father's.

MORE [Trying to take in the exact sense of her words]
Good! You prefer that to an hotel? [**KATHERINE** nods. Gently] Will you let me say, Kit, how terribly I feel for you—Hubert's—

KATHERINE
Don't. I ought to have made what I meant plainer. I am not coming back.

MORE
Not? Not while the house—

KATHERINE
Not—at all.

MORE
Kit!

KATHERINE
I warned you from the first. You've gone too far!

MORE [Terribly moved]
Do you understand what this means? After ten years—and all—our love!

KATHERINE
Was it love? How could you ever have loved one so unheroic as myself!

MORE
This is madness, Kit—Kit!

KATHERINE
Last night I was ready. You couldn't. If you couldn't then, you never can. You are very exalted, Stephen. I don't like living—I won't live, with one whose equal I am not. This has been coming ever since you made that speech. I told you that night what the end would be.

MORE [Trying to put his arms round her]
Don't be so terribly cruel!

KATHERINE
No! Let's have the truth! People so wide apart don't love! Let me go!

MORE
In God's name, how can I help the difference in our faiths?

KATHERINE

Last night you used the word—bargain. Quite right. I meant to buy you. I meant to kill your faith. You showed me what I was doing. I don't like to be shown up as a driver of bargains, Stephen.

MORE

God knows—I never meant—

KATHERINE

If I'm not yours in spirit—I don't choose to be your—mistress.

MORE, as if lashed by a whip, has thrown up his hands in an attitude of defence.

KATHERINE

Yes, that's cruel! It shows the heights you live on. I won't drag you down.

MORE

For God's sake, put your pride away, and see! I'm fighting for the faith that's in me. What else can a man do? What else? Ah! Kit! Do see!

KATHERINE

I'm strangled here! Doing nothing—sitting silent—when my brothers are fighting, and being killed. I shall try to go out nursing. Helen will come with me. I have my faith, too; my poor common love of country. I can't stay here with you. I spent last night on the floor—thinking—and I know!

MORE

And Olive?

KATHERINE

I shall leave her at Father's, with Nurse; unless you forbid me to take her. You can.

MORE [Icily]

That I shall not do—you know very well. You are free to go, and to take her.

KATHERINE [Very low]

Thank you!

[Suddenly she turns to him, and draws his eyes on her. Without a sound, she puts her whole strength into that look.

Stephen! Give it up! Come down to me!

[The festive sounds from the street grow louder. There can be heard the blowing of whistles, and bladders, and all the sounds of joy.

MORE

And drown in—that?

[**KATHERINE** turns swiftly to the door. There she stands and again looks at him. Her face is mysterious, from the conflicting currents of her emotions.

MORE
So—you're going?

KATHERINE [In a whisper]
Yes.

[She bends her head, opens the door, and goes. **MORE** starts forward as if to follow her, but **OLIVE** has appeared in the doorway. She has on a straight little white coat and a round white cap.

OLIVE
Aren't you coming with us, Daddy?

[**MORE** shakes his head.

OLIVE
Why not?

MORE
Never mind, my dicky bird.

OLIVE
The motor'll have to go very slow. There are such a lot of people in the street. Are you staying to stop them setting the house on fire?

[**MORE** nods.

May I stay a little, too?

[**MORE** shakes his head.

Why?

MORE [Putting his hand on her head]
Go along, my pretty!

OLIVE
Oh! love me up, Daddy!

[**MORE** takes and loves her up.

OLIVE
Oo-o!

MORE
Trot, my soul!

[She goes, looks back at him, turns suddenly, and vanishes.

[**MORE** follows her to the door, but stops there. Then, as full realization begins to dawn on him, he runs to the bay window, craning his head to catch sight of the front door. There is the sound of a vehicle starting, and the continual hooting of its horn as it makes its way among the crowd. He turns from the window.

MORE
Alone as the last man on earth!

[Suddenly a voice rises clear out of the hurly-burly in the street.

VOICE
There 'e is! That's 'im! More! Traitor! More!

[A shower of nutshells, orange-peel, and harmless missiles begins to rattle against the glass of the window. Many voices take up the groaning: "More! Traitor! Black-leg! More!" And through the window can be seen waving flags and lighted Chinese lanterns, swinging high on long bamboos. The din of execration swells. **MORE** stands unheeding, still gazing after the cab. Then, with a sharp crack, a flung stone crashes through one of the panes. It is followed by a hoarse shout of laughter, and a hearty groan. A second stone crashes through the glass. **MORE** turns for a moment, with a contemptuous look, towards the street, and the flare of the Chinese lanterns lights up his face. Then, as if forgetting all about the din outside, he moves back into the room, looks round him, and lets his head droop. The din rises louder and louder; a third stone crashes through. **MORE** raises his head again, and, clasping his hands, looks straight before him. The footman, **HENRY**, entering, hastens to the French windows.

MORE
Ah! Henry, I thought you'd gone.

FOOTMAN
I came back, sir.

MORE
Good fellow!

FOOTMAN
They're trying to force the terrace gate, sir. They've no business coming on to private property—no matter what!

[In the surging entrance of the mob the footman, **HENRY**, who shows fight, is overwhelmed, hustled out into the crowd on the terrace, and no more seen. The **MOB** is a mixed crowd of revellers of both sexes, medical students, clerks, shop men and girls, and a Boy Scout or two. Many have exchanged hats— Some wear masks, or false noses, some carry feathers or tin whistles. Some, with bamboos and Chinese lanterns, swing them up outside on the terrace. The medley of noises is very great. Such ringleaders as exist in the confusion are a **GROUP OF STUDENTS**, the chief of whom, conspicuous because unadorned, is an athletic, hatless young man with a projecting underjaw, and heavy coal-black moustache, who seems with the swing of his huge arms and shoulders to sway the currents of motion. When the first surge of noise and movement subsides, he calls out: "To him, boys! Chair the hero!" **THE STUDENTS** rush at the impassive **MORE**, swing him roughly on to their shoulders and bear him round the room. When they have twice circled the table to the music of their confused singing, groans and whistling, **THE CHIEF OF THE STUDENTS** calls out: "Put him down!" Obediently they set him down on the table which has been forced into the bay window, and stand gaping up at him.

CHIEF STUDENT
Speech! Speech!

[The noise ebbs, and **MORE** looks round him.

CHIEF STUDENT
Now then, you, sir.

MORE [In a quiet voice]
Very well. You are here by the law that governs the action of all mobs—the law of Force. By that law, you can do what you like to this body of mine.

A VOICE
And we will, too.

MORE
I don't doubt it. But before that, I've a word to say.

A VOICE
You've always that.

[**ANOTHER VOICE** raises a donkey's braying.

MORE
You—Mob—are the most contemptible thing under the sun. When you walk the street—God goes in.

CHIEF STUDENT
Be careful, you—sir.

VOICES
Down him! Down with the beggar!

MORE [Above the murmurs]
My fine friends, I'm not afraid of you. You've forced your way into my house, and you've asked me to speak. Put up with the truth for once! [His words rush out] You are the thing that pelts the weak; kicks women; howls down free speech. This to-day, and that to-morrow. Brain—you have none. Spirit—not the ghost of it! If you're not meanness, there's no such thing. If you're not cowardice, there is no cowardice [Above the growing fierceness of the hubbub] Patriotism—there are two kinds—that of our soldiers, and this of mine. You have neither!

CHIEF STUDENT [Checking a dangerous rush]
Hold on! Hold on! [To **MORE**] Swear to utter no more blasphemy against your country: Swear it!

CROWD
Ah! Ay! Ah!

MORE
My country is not yours. Mine is that great country which shall never take toll from the weakness of others. [Above the groaning] Ah! you can break my head and my windows; but don't think that you can break my faith. You could never break or shake it, if you were a million to one.

A **GIRL** with dark eyes and hair all wild, leaps out from the crowd and shakes her fist at him.

GIRL
You're friends with them that killed my lad!

[**MORE** smiles down at her, and she swiftly plucks the knife from the belt of a Boy Scout beside her]

Smile, you—cur!

[A violent rush and heave from behind flings **MORE** forward on to the steel. He reels, staggers back, and falls down amongst the crowd. A scream, a sway, a rush, a hubbub of cries. The **CHIEF STUDENT** shouts above the riot: "Steady!" Another: "My God! He's got it!"

CHIEF STUDENT
Give him air!

[The crowd falls back, and two **STUDENTS**, bending over **MORE**, lift his arms and head, but they fall like lead. Desperately they test him for life.

CHIEF STUDENT
By the Lord, it's over!

[Then begins a scared swaying out towards the window. Some one turns out the lights, and in the darkness the crowd fast melts away. The body of **MORE** lies in the gleam from a single Chinese lantern. Muttering the words: "Poor devil! He kept his end up anyway!" the **CHIEF STUDENT** picks from the floor a little abandoned Union Jack and lays it on **MORE's** breast. Then he, too, turns, and rushes out.

And the body of **MORE** lies in the streak of light; and flee noises in the street continue to rise.

THE CURTAIN FALLS, BUT RISES AGAIN ALMOST AT ONCE.

AFTERMATH

A late Spring dawn is just breaking. Against trees in leaf and blossom, with the houses of a London Square beyond, suffused by the spreading glow, is seen a dark life-size statue on a granite pedestal. In front is the broad, dust-dim pavement. The light grows till the central words around the pedestal can be clearly read:

ERECTED
To the Memory of
STEPHEN MORE
"Faithful to his ideal"

High above, the face of **MORE** looks straight before him with a faint smile. On one shoulder and on his bare head two sparrows have perched, and from the gardens, behind, comes the twittering and singing of birds.

THE CURTAIN FALLS.

John Galsworthy – A Short Biography

John Galsworthy, eldest son of John Galsworthy (1817-1904), a solicitor and company director of Old Jewry, London, and Blanche Bailey (1835-1915), daughter of Charles Bartleet, a needlemaker in Redditch. His father's ancestors originated in Wembury, near Plymouth in England, and Galsworthy, for whom family origins were of significant importance, maintained a close connection with Devon. His more immediate family were considerably wealthy and well established in the shipping industry, and owned a fine estate in Kingston-upon-Thames called Parkfield, where Galsworthy was born on the 14th August 1867. At the age of nine he began education at Saugeen, a Bournemouth preparatory school, before starting at Harrow school in 1881 where he remained until 1886, distinguishing himself as an athlete.

His education at Harrow being successful enough to gain him entrance to Oxford, he began at New College to read law and gained a second-class degree with honours in 1889. Following Lincoln's Inn he was called to the bar in 1890. Despite this recognition he realised that he was not keen to actually begin practising law and so he resolved instead to look after the family's shipping business while specialising himself in Marine Law. This decision saw him take to the seas to destinations such as Vancouver, Island and South AFrica, though it was at the age of twenty-five on one particular journey to Australia, motivated by an (unfulfilled) intention to meet Robert Louis Stevenson on Samoa that he would being to realise fully his literary interests: though he was not considering becoming a writer at this time, his enjoyment of literature was enough to encourage an attempt at meeting a great writer and eventually enabled one of the most significant encounters of his life. He made the journey with his friend Edward Sanderson and, though he missed Stevenson, he met Joseph Conrad, a fellow future author famed for his novels which were often nautically themed. At the time Conrad was the first mate of the sailing-ship Torrens moored in the harbour of Adelaide, Australia; still very much focused on his ship-borne career, he was yet to begin his writing in earnest.

Indeed, though neither knew at the time, both Conrad and Galsworthy were at similar junctures in their lives, their time spent as sea acting as a transitional period during which each found their literary calling. It is perhaps owning to this unknown common ground that they became close friends. During his time on the Torrens Galsworthy recorded several details, offering a frank and valuable characterisation of Conrad while also illuminating his own experiences as a student of Marine Law.

"I supposed to be studying navigation for the Admiralty Bar, would every day work out the position of the ship with the captain. On one side of the saloon table we would sit and check our observations with those of Conrad, who from the other side of the table would look at us a little quizzically."

On his return to England and the cessation of his nautical voyaging, Galsworthy began an affair with the wife of his first cousin, Major Arthur John Galsworthy. Ada Nemesis Pearson Cooper (1864-1956), the daughter of Emanuel Copper, an obstetrician from Norwich, remained married to the Major for ten years and the affair remained secret for its duration. In order to conceal the affair they took considerable pains to avoid suspicion. One such tactic was to stay in a secluded farmhouse called Wingstone in the village on Manaton on Dartmoor, in Devon. In Galsworthy's decision to choose Devon as the location for their clandestine rendezvous we see evidence of Galsworthy's affection for the place of his father's origin. It was only when, in 1905, she divorced the Major that their affair became known following their marriage on 23rd September of that year.

Galsworthy now took to writing sometime after having met Conrad and his career began in earnest when, in 1897, his first work, From the Four Winds, a volume of short stories, was published under the pseudonym John Sinjohn. He succeeded this in 1898 with Jocelyn, his first novel, and then his second in 1900, Villa Rubein. In 1901 he published a second volume of short stories, A Man of Devon, which was the last of his work to be published under pseudonym. The first of his work to be published under his own name was The Island Pharisees in 1904, a novel of social observation, seasoned with flashes of satire and propaganda. His decision to write under his own name is arguably owing to the recent death of his father, either as a mark of respect to his name or because now he was able to publish freely without incurring the possibility of paternal disappointment at his choice of career. It also marked a shift in his professionalism; he had hitherto published with small, independent publishers, but The Island Pharisees was published by Heinemann, a far more established House and one with whom he remained for the duration of his writing career.

He arguably cemented his position and maturity as a writer when, in 1906, he saw the publication of both his first major play, The Silver Box, and the novel The Man of Property. Each was published to considerable critical acclaim, and to achieve both in such a short space of time was impressive. the Silver Box concerns the imbalance in the justice system with regards to criminals of differing class by contrasting the treatment of a poor thief and a rich thief, both of whom stole silver cigarette cases but for very different reasons. The complexity of individual experience when not dealt with in public is highlighted and questioned in a bravely critical manner; despite the clear issues it raises with class and privilege, the final night was attended by the Price and Princess of Wales. The Man of Property was the first novel in the famous The Forsyte Saga, a trilogy of novels with an 'interlude' between each one, written between 1906 and 1921. Dealing with the questions of status, class and materialism, The Man of Property introduces us to the Forsyte family, particularly Soames Forsyte, who is acutely aware of his status as 'new money' and equally keen to assert himself as a wealthy man. Jealous of his wife and desperate to own things in order to confirm his wealth to those observing him, he engineers a plan to keep his wife from her friends which backfires spectacularly when, instead of cutting her off, all Soames achieves is enabling her to have an affair. This drives Soames to terrible actions with terrible consequences, which Galsworthy depicts with confidence.

Very typically Edwardian, the novel focuses on conflict between property and art, and to a certain degree much of its emotional power is drawn from Galsworthy's own life, particularly his affair with Ada. Their rendezvous in the countryside of Devon mirror the manner in which Forsyte seeks to relocate his wife and; though theirs was a much healthier relationship, there are clear similarities. By examining the fragile nature of the class system and those moving within it Galsworthy offered an important perspective on the relationships between material wealth, personal happiness and obsession, and the manner in which these change over time. His contemporaries widely regarded the publication of this novel as marking the end of Victorianism. His friend Conrad praised it as "indubitably a piece of art" and, though the notoriously risqué D.H. Lawrence lamented the novel's timidity in the face of sexuality and sensuality, he considered it potentially "a very great novel, a very great satire".

Though he continued to write both plays and novels, it was his work as a playwright for which he was most celebrated by his contemporaries. Indeed, his next novel, The Country House, seems uncharacteristically unfocused, its satirical view of those belonging to the country set comparatively unremarkable and weakly characterised, while at times the tone of satire becomes one of ironic detachment. In 1909 he published Fraternity, an exploration of of the various connections between urban society and the social classes therein, though its representation of lower-class Londoners is utterly unconvincing and ill-informed. Remaining with the subject of the landed gentry and the society surrounding it, in 1915 he published The Freelands, which does not stray far from conservative discussions of capitalism, the rural economy and their interrelationship.

His drama, however, featured a convincingly muted realism, directed at a relatively small, educated and politically-aware audience. His social agenda is prevalent here too, and is represented in a simple and static manner producing arresting instances of high drama. This talent for creating moments of captivating theatre is complimented by an instinctual sense of balance enabling his narratives to vacillate between their emotional high- and low-points, ultimately reaching conclusive equilibrium. This is particularly evident in one of his most popular plays, Strife, published in 1909 and examining the antagonists in a strike at a Cornish tin mine. In this, and in 1910's Justice, he approaches his subject with sympathy, irony and balance, which establishes a position of narrative authority while garnering the audiences trust that he is representing his characters and their motives justly. Justice condemns the use of solitary confinement in prisons, a reformist agenda which caught the liberality of his contemporary audiences along with the home secretary, Winston Churchill. Despite he was careful to disassociate himself with politics and professed himself apolitical, he and his work were nevertheless aligned with the views of the Liberal establishment. He spent much of the duration of the First World War working in a field hospital in France as an orderly having been passed over for military service.

Despite the popularity and brilliance of his work, it was only in 1920 that he had his first true commercial success with The Skin Game, a melodrama dealing with ethics, property and class. The play was adapted by Alfred Hitchcock in 1931. Galsworthy, meanwhile, had turned down a knighthood in 1918, considering his work not sufficient to be made a knight of the realm. He did, however, accept the Belgian Palmes d'Or in the following year. In 1920 he published the second novel in the Forsyte Saga, In Chancery, in which he resumes many of the themes of the first novel, focusing on the marital disharmony between Soames Forsyte and his wife. Katherine Mansfield considered it "a fascinating, brilliant book" in her review in The Atheneum. Then, in 1921, he was elected as the PEN International Literary Club's first president. The concluding novel to The Forsyte Saga, To Let was published in 1921 with a kind of peace being found between Forsyte and his now-ex wife, though he is left contemplating his losses and his greed. More ironic treatment of class confusions followed in Loyalties, bringing with it more popular success which lasted until 1926 and Escape, the last of his popular plays. Though he enjoyed popular success it was inconsistent and relatively small. His Collected Plays was published in 1929.

Over the course of time the appreciation of his work has gradually shifted from his plays to his novels, and particularly the detail and intricacy of his chronicle of English social difference, tension and pretension in The Forsyte Saga. Its success encouraged Galsworthy to revisit Soames Forsyte in a second trilogy, A Modern Comedy, which follows Soames's obsessive love of his daughter Fleur. In its three volumes, The White Monkey (1924), The Silver Spoon (1936) and Swan Song (1928) he examines the English commercial upper-middle class and its ideologies, its instinct to possess as its only way of distinguishing itself manifested in the poisonous materialism of Soames. Interestingly, this emergent social class which he so vehemently criticises is the very class from which he emerged. He witnessed first-hand its insularity, its chauvinism, its restrictive and oppressive morality, its stubborn imperialism and its materialism, and it is this experience which enables him to write so comfortably about it. Swan Song is widely considered among the best of Galsworthy's writing for the depth of its exploration of society and its heightened emotional subtlety. In 1929 he was appointed to the Order of Merit, despite having turned down a knighthood earlier. He spent his last years writing a third trilogy, End of the Chapter, beginning in 1931 with Maid in Waiting, Flowering Wilderness in 1932 and concluding with Over The River in 1933. These are significantly less coherent works and are indicative of his deteriorating health. Indeed, in 1932 he was awarded the Nobel Prize, though he was too ill to attend the ceremony.

Throughout the course of his career he received honorary degrees from the universities of St Andrews (1922), Manchester (1927), Dublin (1929), Cambridge (1930), Sheffield (1930), Oxford (1931), and Princeton (1931). In 1926 New College, Oxford, elected him as an honourary fellow. In photographs he is portrayed as handsome, fastidiously dressed and dignified. He was unusually compassionate and this saw him involved in several charitable and humane causes throughout the course of his life, including penal reforms, attacks on theatrical censorship and campaigning for animal rights. Though he spent the majority of the final seven years of his life at his home in Bury, West Sussex, it was at his home in Hampstead, London, that he died of a brain tumour on 31st January, 1933, six weeks after having been too ill to attend the ceremony in honour of his receiving the Nobel Prize. According to demands made in his will he was cremated and his ashes scattered over the South Downs from an aeroplane. Also in his will was his wish to leave cottages to several of his astonished tenants. He is memorialised in Highgate 'New' Cemetery and in the cloisters of New College, Oxford, where he was an honourary fellow.

John Galsworthy – A Concise Bibliography

From the Four Winds, 1897 (as John Sinjohn)
Jocelyn, 1898 (as John Sinjohn)
Villa Rubein, 1900 (as John Sinjohn)
A Man of Devon, 1901 (as John Sinjohn)
The Island Pharisees, 1904
The Silver Box, 1906 (his first play)
The Man of Property, 1906 – First book of The Forsyte Saga (1922)
The Country House, 1907
A Commentary, 1908
Fraternity, 1909
A Justification for the Censorship of Plays, 1909
Strife, 1909
Fraternity, 1909
Joy, 1909

Justice, 1910
A Motley, 1910
The Spirit of Punishment, 1910
Horses in Mines, 1910
The Patrician, 1911
The Little Dream, 1911
The Pigeon, 1912
The Eldest Son, 1912
Quality, 1912
Moods, Songs, and Doggerels, 1912
For Love of Beasts, 1912
The Inn of Tranquillity, 1912
The Dark Flower, 1913
The Fugitive, 1913
The Mob, 1914
The Freelands, 1915
The Little Man, 1915
A Bit o' Love, 1915
A Sheaf, 1916
The Apple Tree, 1916
The Foundations, 1917
Beyond, 1917
Five Tales, 1918
Indian Summer of a Forsyte, 1918 – First interlude of The Forsyte Saga
Saint's Progress, 1919
Addresses in America, 1912
In Chancery, 1920 – Second book of The Forsyte Saga
Awakening, 1920 – Second interlude of The Forsyte Saga
The Skin Game, 1920
To Let, 1921 – Third book of The Forsyte Saga
A Family Man, 1922
The Little Man, 1922
Loyalties, 1922
Windows, 1922
Captures, 1923
Abracadabra, 1924
The Forest, 1924
Old English, 1924
The White Monkey, 1924 – First book of A Modern Comedy (1929)
The Show, 1925
Escape, 1926
The Silver Spoon, 1926 – Second book of A Modern Comedy
Verses New and Old, 1926
Castles in Spain, 1927
A Silent Wooing, 1927 – First Interlude of A Modern Comedy
Passers By, 1927 – Second Interlude of A Modern Comedy
Swan Song, 1928 – Third book of A Modern Comedy
The Manaton Edition, 1923–26 (collection, 30 vols.)

Exiled, 1929
The Roof, 1929
On Forsyte 'Change, 1930
Two Essays on Conrad, 1930
Soames and the Flag, 1930
The Creation of Character in Literature, 1931 (The Romanes Lecture for 1931).
Maid in Waiting, 1931 – First book of End of the Chapter (1934)
Forty Poems, 1932
Flowering Wilderness, 1932 – Second book of End of the Chapter
Autobiographical Letters of Galsworthy: A Correspondence with Frank Harris, 1933
One More River (originally Over the River), 1933 – Third book of End of the Chapter
The Grove Edition, 1927–34 (collection, 27 Vols.)
Collected Poems, 1934
Punch and Go, 1935
The Life and Letters, 1935
The Winter Garden, 1935
Forsytes, Pendyces and Others, 1935
Selected Short Stories, 1935
Glimpses and Reflections, 1937
Galsworthy's Letters to Leon Lion, 1968
Letters from John Galsworthy 1900–1932, 1970
Caravan the assembled tales of John Galsworthy, New York Charles Scribner's Sons 1925

www.ingramcontent.com/pod-product-compliance
Lightning Source LLC
Chambersburg PA
CBHW060147050426
42448CB00010B/2341